W9-BIY-086

THE SCIENCE BEHIND
NATURAL PHENOMENA

THE SCIENCE BEHIND

WONDERS OF THE
WATER

EXPLODING LAKES, ICE CIRCLES, AND BRINICLES

BY SUZANNE GARBE

CONSULTANT:
DR. SANDRA MATHER
PROFESSOR EMERITA, DEPARTMENT OF GEOLOGY AND ASTRONOMY,
WEST CHESTER UNIVERSITY, WEST CHESTER, PENNSYLVANIA

CAPSTONE PRESS
a capstone imprint

Edge Books are published by Capstone Press,
1710 Roe Crest Drive, North Mankato, Minnesota 56003
www.mycapstone.com

Copyright © 2017 by Capstone Press, a Capstone imprint. All rights reserved.
No part of this publication may be reproduced in whole or in part, or stored in a
retrieval system, or transmitted in any form or by any means, electronic, mechanical,
photocopying, recording, or otherwise, without written permission of the publisher.

Library of Congress Cataloging-in-Publication Data
Names: Garbe, Suzanne, author.
Title: The science behind wonders of the water : exploding lakes, ice
circles, and brinicles / by Suzanne Garbe.
Description: North Mankato, Minnesota : Capstone Press, [2017] | Series: Edge
books. The science behind natural phenomena | Audience: Ages 9—15. |
Audience: Grades 4 to 6. | Includes bibliographical references and index.
Identifiers: LCCN 2016005757| ISBN 9781515707769 (library binding) | ISBN
9781515707813 (paperback) | ISBN 9781515707851 (ebook (pdf))
Subjects: LCSH: Hydrology—Juvenile literature. | Oceanography—Juvenile literature.
Classification: LCC GB662.3 .G36 2017 | DDC 551.4802—dc23
LC record available at http://lccn.loc.gov/2016005757

Editorial Credits
Linda Staniford, editor; Terri Poburka, designer;
Svetlana Zhurkin, media researcher; Katy LaVigne, production specialist

Photo Credits
Corbis: Louise Gubb, 9; Getty Images: Gamma-Rapho/Eric Bouvet, 7; iStockphoto:
Onfokus, 10; Minden Pictures: Chadden Hunter, 23; NASA: JPL, 14–15; Newscom:
Xinhua News Agency/Han Chuanhao, 28, ZUMA Press/UPPA, 29; Shutterstock:
BS_Lexx, 5 (inset), daulon, 25, dikobraziy, 24–25, dovla982, 8, elnavegante, 5, Gabriele
Maltinti, 12, kavram, cover, mapichai, 13, mTaira, 26–27, Peter Hermes Furian, 16–17
(back), posteriori, 19, PSD photography, 18, rook76, 16 (inset), Shaiith, 21 (back),
Vadim Petrakov, 17 (inset), VikaSuh, 1 and throughout; Wikimedia: U.S. Coast Guard,
21 (inset)

Printed and bound in China
007702

TABLE OF
CONTENTS

THE WONDERS OF WATER

All around the world, humans are drawn to water. We build sand castles beside the sea. We go fishing on lakes. We take rafting trips on rivers. We splash, surf, and sail.

In the water, though, new marvels are waiting. Humans have explored less than 5 percent of the undersea world. There is much about the ocean we don't yet know. However, what we do know already is truly amazing.

Water holds wonders that are both beautiful and frightening. It awes us with underwater icicles and waterfalls. It surprises us with natural, perfect circles of ice in a river. It scares us with waves big enough to wipe out entire cities.

How do such amazing wonders occur? Scientists have studied many of these natural **phenomena**. For some, they have found logical explanations. For others, the scientific explanation has yet to be discovered.

How Much Freshwater is on Earth?

Only 3 percent of the water on Earth is **freshwater.** Most of it is locked in glaciers and the polar ice caps. The water we can actually use for drinking is less than 1 percent of all the water on Earth. The rest is seawater, which contains salt and other minerals. Seawater can be made safe to drink only through a very expensive and difficult process.

phenomenon—an unusual or remarkable event

freshwater—water containing only tiny amounts of salt and other minerals, like the water found in most lakes and streams, and the water we drink

EXPLODING LAKES

Before August 21, 1986, most people outside Cameroon in West Africa knew nothing about Lake Nyos. The lake lies in the crater of an old volcano. It is located about 200 miles (322 kilometers) from Yaoundé, the capital of Cameroon.

The night of August 21, most people living near the lake were asleep. But a few people who were awake noticed something strange about the lake. The water took on a reddish brown color. Large waves formed. Then a cloud of gas exploded from the lake. People noticed a bad smell. Many people suffered breathing problems and went to the hospital for treatment. However, others weren't so lucky. More than 1,700 people died.

After the explosion the water in Lake Nyos turned brown, and the water level dropped.

Scientists swarmed to the lake. They learned the **extinct** volcano was releasing carbon dioxide. That gas, which is heavier than water, had been building up on the lake's floor. Before the explosion, the area had experienced heavy rains. Scientists believe the cool rain water mixed with the warmer lake water and disturbed the gas at the bottom of the lake. This made the carbon dioxide rise and explode from the lake.

extinct—no longer capable of erupting

The huge death toll from the explosion prompted scientists to begin studying the phenomenon. To keep it from happening again, French **engineers** installed a huge pipe from the layer of gas on the lake floor to the surface. The pipe carries water and small amounts of carbon dioxide to the surface. Removing the carbon dioxide in small amounts isn't dangerous.

The explosion also led to a study of other lakes throughout Africa. Scientists now know of two other lakes that could explode like Lake Nyos. One of them, Lake Monoun, which is near Lake Nyos, exploded in 1984, killing 37 people. A similar pipe has been installed there that has removed much of the dangerous gas from the lake.

The other lake that could explode, Lake Kivu in Rwanda, has not exploded. Scientists viewed the gas there not just as a threat, but also as an opportunity. They have found a way to capture the gas and use it to power nearby homes.

Cameroon

Rwanda

engineer—someone trained to design and build machines, vehicles, bridges, roads, or other structures

Carbon dioxide is released from beneath Lake Nyos through this pipe. Scientists collect samples of the water to check the gas levels.

AMAZING FACT

Carbon dioxide is a natural gas produced by humans and other animals when breathing out. In small doses, carbon dioxide is safe.

ICE CIRCLES

In 2013 George Loegering was hunting in North Dakota when he stumbled across something astonishing. In a bend of the Sheyenne River was a perfectly formed circle of ice about 55 feet (17 meters) across. Even more surprisingly, the ice circle was slowly rotating in the river.

Ice circles are probably formed when a burst of unusually cold air causes ice to form on a fast-flowing river. On a curve in the river, the water flows faster, making an **eddy**. If the ice is caught in an eddy, pieces can break off. They spin in the river's current, forming a circle.

Although ice circles appear to be solid sheets of ice, they are actually a collection of pieces of ice. The ice in the circle rubs against other pieces of ice floating by. That **friction** causes the ice to get worn down and shaped into a perfect circle.

Ice circles aren't common. They usually form in places with very cold climates, such as the Arctic, Canada, and Scandinavia. However, when conditions are right, they are occasionally spotted in parts of the United States and Great Britain.

eddy—a circular current in water or air

friction—a force produced when two objects rub against each other; friction slows down objects

THE OCEAN'S CONVEYOR BELT

One of the least understood parts of the ocean is the slow movement of water around the world. This "conveyor belt" carries water from the surface to the depths of the ocean floor and back again. It moves water from one ocean to another, across the entire planet.

Warm surface currents flow toward the North Pole in the Northern Hemisphere.

Cold currents in the Northern Hemisphere sink and flow south into the deep oceans.

In the North Atlantic Ocean, near the North Pole, the winter darkness can last more than five months. This long winter darkness results in an extreme cold that freezes freshwater in the ocean where it lies near land. As the freshwater freezes, salt is removed from it. The surrounding water becomes saltier. The cold temperatures and high salt levels affect the **density** of the water. If one area of water is more dense than another area, the denser water weighs more and sinks. The cold, salty water then sinks toward the ocean floor.

density—the amount of mass an object or substance has based on a unit of volume

As cold water sinks near the North Pole, it is replaced by warmer water from the equator. The cold water then moves across the ocean floor. The **topography** of the ocean floor and changes in temperature and **salinity** cause the water to continue moving. Above the ocean, wind also causes waves that move water near the surface.

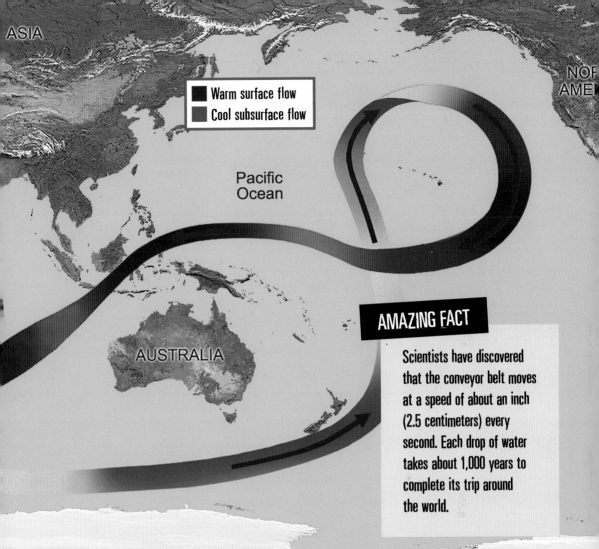

ASIA

NORTH
AMERICA

Warm surface flow
Cool subsurface flow

Pacific
Ocean

AUSTRALIA

AMAZING FACT

Scientists have discovered that the conveyor belt moves at a speed of about an inch (2.5 centimeters) every second. Each drop of water takes about 1,000 years to complete its trip around the world.

Oxygen, carbon dioxide, and nutrients travel through the water as it moves around the world. They provide food for tiny plants and animals that live in the ocean. These plants and animals are the base of the world's food chain. All other living things depend on them to survive.

topography—shapes and forms of land in a particular area; includes mountains, valleys, plains, lakes, and rivers

salinity—the level of salt in a liquid

UNDERWATER WATERFALLS

We often imagine the floor of the ocean as a flat, peaceful place. But it's not. Under the world's oceans is a wild **terrain** of mountains, valleys, and hills.

On land if a river reaches a cliff or other sharp drop in its path, a waterfall is formed. What happens underwater if a dense, heavy current encounters a steep cliff? An underwater waterfall!

The largest known underwater waterfall is the Denmark Strait waterfall. It lies between Iceland and Greenland. It's 2.2 miles (3.5 km) high. That makes it more than three times as tall as the tallest waterfall on land, Venezuela's Angel Falls. Angel Falls is just 0.6 miles (1 km) high.

The Denmark Strait waterfall also moves an impressive amount of water. Each second 1.3 billion gallons (5 billion liters) of water rush over the waterfall. The Bioyoma Falls in the Democratic Republic of the Congo moves more water per second than any other waterfall on land. But the Denmark Strait underwater waterfall moves nearly 400 times more water each second!

terrain—an area of land and its physical features

Angel Falls,
Venezuela, is the
highest waterfall
on land.

*Venezuela's
Angel Falls
waterfall is
0.6 miles
(1 km) high.*

*The Denmark
Strait waterfall
is 2.2 miles
(3.5 km) high.*

Greenland

**Denmark
Strait
waterfall**

Iceland

AMAZING FACT

Earth's longest mountain range and deepest valley are also found
underwater. The longest mountain range is called the Mid-Atlantic
Ridge. The deepest valley is the Mariana Trench.

ICEBERGS

Icebergs are a fascinating part of our planet's water cycle. They form when a chunk of ice breaks off a **glacier**, or another iceberg. For a piece of ice to be an iceberg, it must rise at least 16 feet (5 m) above the ocean's surface. It must also be 98 to 164 feet (30 to 50 m) thick and have an area of at least 5,382 square feet (500 square m). Icebergs can look large and impressive above the surface. However, most of an iceberg is actually hidden underwater.

After an iceberg is formed, currents carry it to new, warmer places. As warm air melts the ice on the surface, the water forms ponds. These ponds cause the iceberg to crack and split into smaller pieces. The warm ocean water also starts to melt the sides and bottom of the iceberg. The iceberg will gradually break into smaller pieces and melt into the ocean.

A huge stack of ice breaks off a glacier to form an iceberg.

AMAZING FACT

In Greenland the weather is so cold that icebergs exist all year round. They are constant features, like hills and mountains. People once identified towns by the icebergs that were near them.

glacier—a huge moving body of ice found in mountain valleys or polar regions

Icebergs are made up of freshwater. This is because the glaciers they break off of were originally formed by rain and snow. As icebergs move through the ocean and melt, they add freshwater to the ocean. Freshwater is less dense than seawater. It cannot sink to the ocean floor and circulate through the deep ocean. Melting icebergs can affect ocean currents and even slow the ocean's conveyor belt.

Icebergs are also interesting to scientists who study climate change. Climate change is making our planet warmer. No one is sure how that will impact glaciers and ice shelves. However, we do know how icebergs react when they move through the ocean into warm areas. Studying this process helps scientists predict how glaciers might react to global warming.

In the 100 years that scientists have been tracking icebergs, the largest one found was called B-15. It was the size of Connecticut. It **calved** off an ice shelf in Antarctica in 2000. Fourteen years later pieces of the iceberg still floated around the Antarctic.

calving—the act of a piece of ice breaking off an iceberg or glacier

Icebergs are white because of the way snow and ice reflect light. Occasionally, icebergs flip over, revealing a glassy, blue underside. This blue ice is formed when oxygen is squeezed from the ice by pressure as water melts the iceberg from below.

International Ice Patrol

When the *Titanic* sank in 1912, it wasn't the first ship to go down after hitting an iceberg. But it was the biggest. At the time, the *Titanic* was the largest passenger ship ever built. Some people thought it was unsinkable. However, it sank on its very first voyage. People around the world then realized how deadly icebergs could be. As a result the United States, Great Britain, Canada, and 10 other countries created the International Ice Patrol. The International Ice Patrol first used ships, and now uses aircraft, to track icebergs in the North Atlantic Ocean.

A U.S. Coast Guard Ice Patrol aircraft flies past an iceberg in the Arctic Ocean.

21

BRINICLES

A brinicle forms under the ice and grows toward the sea floor.

Icicles are common in winter. They can form when water dripping from a roof freezes into an icy spear. But have you ever heard of an underwater icicle? It seems impossible, right? But it's not!

Salty water is called **brine**. A brine icicle, or brinicle, forms when unusually salty brine drips from an iceberg or ice sheet. The saltier water is, the heavier it is. This makes brine sink.

Brine has a lower freezing point than freshwater. This means that even below freezing, it's still a liquid. If the brine is colder than freezing, the less salty ocean water it touches will freeze. As the brine sinks, the icicle forming around it gets longer and longer. If the ocean is shallow, the brinicle can reach the ocean floor and spread a thin layer of ice across the floor. Fish or other creatures can get trapped in the ice and die.

AMAZING FACT

On average, the ocean is 3.5 percent salt. That salt comes from rocks and soil on land as well as from the ocean floor. As rain falls on Earth, it carries salt and other minerals to streams, rivers, and ultimately out to sea.

brine—salty water

TSUNAMIS

One of the ocean's most frightening and dangerous phenomena is the **tsunami**. Tsunamis are a series of ocean waves that can move as fast as a jet. They reach speeds of 480 miles (750 km) per hour. As they approach land, they can grow to a height of more than 100 feet (30 m). That's as tall as a 10-story building!

Tsunamis are caused when a large amount of ocean water is **displaced** by an underwater earthquake, volcanic eruption, or underwater landslide. They can also be caused by events above the water. For example, a huge iceberg falling off a glacier can trigger a tsunami. After an earthquake scientists can determine where a tsunami might strike and issue a tsunami warning.

Tsunamis can last for hours. In 1979 an earthquake near Colombia caused a tsunami that traveled across the Pacific Ocean for 19 hours. The wave traveled as far as Hawaii and Japan.

The 1979 tsunami traveled from Colombia across the Pacific Ocean to Hawaii and Japan.

Japan

Hawaii

tsunami traveling toward land

ocean water displaced

underwater earthquake

AMAZING FACT

Tsunami is a Japanese word. It combines "tsu," or *harbor*, with "nami," or *wave*. Of course, tsunamis can hit anywhere on shore, not just in harbors.

STATES

Columbia

displace—to cause something or someone to leave its usual place

tsunami—a series of ocean waves usually caused by an underwater earthquake, landslide, or volcanic eruption

Before tsunamis reach land, they are spread
out. A tsunami can spread out for 300 miles
(500 km). At this point a tsunami might only
be 2 feet (0.6 m) high. A tsunami can pass
beneath a ship without the crew noticing.

Tsunamis become dangerous only as
they get close to land. As the ocean becomes
shallower, the waves often get taller. In other
cases the tsunami might not approach land
as a tall wall of water. Instead, it might surge
inland like a very fast-moving tide, quickly
covering coastal areas of land.

AMADING FACT

One of the worst tsunamis in recorded history was the Indian Ocean tsunami of 2004. It killed nearly 230,000 people.

As a tsunami moves, its force sucks water in toward it. When that happens, water **recedes** from shore. Shipwrecks and other forgotten objects might be visible for the first time. People who recognize this as the sign of a tsunami have less than five minutes to run for safety. Then the water comes rushing back towards the shore. It is accompanied by a loud roar. As the tsunami hits land, it breaks trees, destroys houses, and sweeps away cars. One tsunami can include five to ten separate waves that arrive over several hours.

recede—to move back and away from something

TIDAL BORES

Sometimes ocean waves push their way up into rivers. These tidal **bores** occur where rivers enter oceans. For tidal bores to occur, the river needs to be the right size and shape. One condition that affects tidal bores is the river's width. If the river narrows, the wave gets pressed into a smaller space. This makes the wave taller and stronger. There are around 60 places in the world where tidal bores regularly form. In some of these places, tidal bores happen every day. In others they only happen when the tide is strongest. This is usually when there is a full moon or a new moon.

Most tidal bores are very small. The waves might be only 8 inches (20 cm) tall. But elsewhere they can be huge. The largest regular tidal bore, found in China, is called the Silver Dragon. It can be more than 29 feet (8.9 m) tall. The Silver Dragon can move as fast as 25 miles (40 km) per hour.

The Silver Dragon tidal bore in China moves at up to 25 miles (40 km) per hour.

AMAZING FACT

Ocean tides are caused by the pull of gravity from the Moon, Earth, and Sun.

Surfers compete to ride the Severn Bore in Great Britain. The wave moves at more than 10 miles (16 km) per hour.

Another famous tidal bore is on the Severn River in Great Britain. There, tidal bores occur more than 250 times a year. Surfers have been able to ride the Severn Bore as far as 7 miles (11 km) up the river. By contrast, surfers haven't been able to ride the Silver Dragon for longer than 11 seconds.

Tidal bores are just one example of the many amazing phenomena found in Earth's waters. As we continue to explore, who knows what other wonders of water are waiting for us and what scientific explanations will be found for them?

bore—a wall of water made when two bodies of water flow into each other, for example when a tide rushes up a shallow bay or river

Glossary

bore (BOR)—a wall of water made when two bodies of water flow into each other, for example when a tide rushes up a shallow bay or river

brine (BRINE)—salty water

calving (KAHV-ing)—the act of a piece of ice breaking off an iceberg or glacier

density (DEN-si-tee)—the amount of mass an object or substance has based on a unit of volume

displace (diss-PLACE)—to cause something or someone to leave its usual place

eddy (E-dee)—a circular current in water or air

engineer (en-juh-NEER)—someone trained to design and build machines, vehicles, bridges, roads, or other structures

extinct (ik-STINGKT)—no longer capable of erupting

freshwater (FRESH-waw-tur)—water containing only tiny amounts of salt and other minerals, like the water found in most lakes and streams, and the water we drink

friction (FRIK-shuhn)—a force produced when two objects rub against each other; friction slows down objects

glacier (GLAY-shur)—a huge moving body of ice found in mountain valleys or polar regions

phenomenon (fe-NOM-uh-non)—an unusual or remarkable event

recede (ree-SEED)—to move back and away from something

salinity (suh-LIN-uh-tee)—the level of salt in a liquid

terrain (TER-rain)—an area of land and its physical features

topography (tuh-PAWG-ruh-fee)—shapes and forms of land in a particular area; includes mountains, valleys, plains, lakes, and rivers

tsunami (tsoo-NAH-mee)—a series of ocean waves usually caused by an underwater earthquake, landslide, or volcanic eruption

Read More

Fertig, Dennis. *Sylvia Earle: Ocean Explorer.* Women in Conservation. Mankato, Minn.: Capstone Press, 2015.

Hague, Bradley. *Alien Deep: Revealing the Mysterious Living World at the Bottom of the Ocean.* Washington, D.C.: National Geographic, 2012.

Hunter, Nick. *Seas.* Explorer Travel Guides. Chicago: Capstone Raintree, 2014.

Woodward, John. *Ocean: A Visual Encyclopedia.* New York: DK Publishing, 2015.

Internet Sites

FactHound offers a safe, fun way to find Internet sites related to this book. All of the sites on FactHound have been researched by our staff.

Here's all you do:

Visit *www.facthound.com*

Type in this code: 9781515707769

 Check out projects, games and lots more at **www.capstonekids.com**

Critical Thinking Using the Common Core

1. Explain how a brinicle is formed. (Key Ideas and Details)
2. Describe the events that happen after an earthquake triggers a tsunami. (Craft and Structure)
3. Why do you think it is important to life on Earth that oxygen, carbon dioxide, and nutrients are carried around the world by the ocean conveyor belt? (Integration of Knowledge and Ideas)

Index